LITTLE BOXES

A tribute to a disappearing railway icon

Written and illustrated by Roger Elsom

First published in 2023 by Transport Treasury Publishing Ltd., 16 Highworth Close, High Wycombe HP13 7PJ

ISBN: 978 1 91528 10 29

An imprint of
Transport Treasury Publishing

To my travelling companions Chris, Peter and Ian who, with their mutual concern for the loss of one of Britain's iconic artefacts and their unbounded enthusiasm during our tours of the UK, have all been an inspiration for this book.

Here, beside Saltmarshe station signal box in Yorkshire, my two Ordnance Survey colleagues Ian and Peter are seeking some refreshments from our car in a brief break during one of our UK tours. This was a most rewarding two-day excursion of a 721-mile round-trip from Southampton in glorious spring weather, resulting in us discovering and documenting 58 signal boxes. A lot of miles covered, perhaps, but at just 12 miles per box we considered that to be a good return for our efforts.

My first interest in railways began, like so many other young people, with spotting and collating locomotive numbers. Yes, I was a "train spotter", that gentle and harmless activity that for some reason evokes so much ridicule from certain members of today's public. As an eight year-old lad, during the war in 1943, I acquired my first ABC of the Great Western Region, published by that gentleman with intuitive foresight, Ian Allan, who realised the potential of producing detailed information booklets of all the locomotives then hauling British trains around the country. Thus, an already established and thriving hobby was instantly given much greater impetus. Armed with my ABC, I passed away many a happy hour with my pals at Oldfield Park station in Bath, where I was then living with my grandparents, having been evacuated there from Bristol three years previously. Despite the disruption to everyone's lives in those trying times, rail traffic was, incredibly, still frequent through little Oldfield Park, serving as it did (and still does) trains between Wales and Portsmouth, together with London expresses to and from the West Country. With practically nothing to entertain a bunch of eight year-olds at that time save our own intuition and imagination, it is little wonder that we spent most of our spare time alongside that busy line.

With passing time, my interest in simple train spotting waned, but I never completely lost the lure of the general railway scene. It wasn't until much later however, in the 1970s, that I became aware of one aspect of that scene that was changing significantly – the gradual demise and disappearance of the humble mechanical signal boxes all over the country, due to the introduction of power signalling. During the next few years, several excursions by car with my nephew and a couple of colleagues from work, all armed with cameras, saw us travelling far and wide to capture on film as many of the remaining boxes that we could before they were lost forever. The images in this book are derived directly from some of those photographs or from other publications, my main aim being to produce fairly accurate, architecturally correct pencil drawings, rather than artistic sketches. Having worked as a cartographer for the Ordnance Survey for 44 years, another of my interests, unsurprisingly, is mapping, and my maps here, also hand-drawn, are based on the O.S. 1/50,000 Landranger Series. Having access to the nation's comprehensive library of large-scale plans also proved to be an invaluable asset in locating exactly where the signal boxes were, thus saving much valuable time when we were on the road.

During our travels around the country, we did try to act like responsible adults, but occasionally, to reach a box located in an unapproachable position, at least by normal means, some minor trespass was required on our part. This sometimes resulted in the anticipated angry verbal response from the local landowner, or the signalman himself, advising us to "CLEAR OFF" – or, more likely, much stronger words to that effect! One of our excursions even involved a brush with the police. We had driven in a hire-car to cover the Leicestershire area and, on reaching the station in Leicester, we parked briefly on a double yellow line while one of us hopped out to take a look over a railway bridge to see where the signal boxes were. We could have been there for no more than five minutes before driving on to look for a legal parking place. Back home the next day, I answered a knock on our front door to find two CID officers standing there. Initial questions as to my identity and "was I driving a particular vehicle in Leicester yesterday?" led to the revelation that a member of the public had given our car number to the police, not because we were on a double yellow but, unknown to us, we had stopped outside a particularly sensitive military establishment. Obviously, the sight of a grubby, travel-stained car containing four "shifty" looking characters, had triggered someone's suspicions and sense of duty. It so happened that one of the policemen was a railway enthusiast himself and, after I had explained our reasons for being where we were, he was far more interested in looking through some of my photographs than in taking the matter any further. A few such incidents certainly added spice to our trips, but mostly our presence at the boxes we visited was treated either with complete indifference, amused curiosity or, on some occasions in remote locations, a very welcoming invitation to enter the box by a lonely signalman who was only too glad of some human company to help pass the long hours of inactivity between infrequent train movements.

So, this modest offering to the railway literature scene is derived from a combination of (a) my interest in railways, (b) my career as a cartographer, (c) my deep regret at the loss of yet another aspect of British heritage, and (d) the fact that one of my few natural talents is the ability to create reasonably accomplished images with a pencil.

Roger Elsom
Southampton 2023

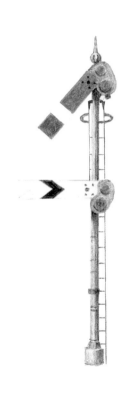

If you are not married when you take over a box, chances are you will never marry.

Frank McKenna, 'The Railway Workers 1840-1970'

LITTLE BOXES

The earliest structures related to signalling and the safe passage of trains were invariably wooden huts designed to provide no more than a rudimentary shelter for the railway "policemen" (as signalmen were first called). Anyone responsible for controlling the trains' movements in those days would spend most of their working hours moving around their patch to show a flag to oncoming trains, operate a signal post capstan to change a signal, or move a lever to change a set of points. As more equipment was introduced, it was found to be more efficient to group signal and point levers together in one place, and the signal box, as we know it today, was first introduced in the 1850s. In the beginning, signal box construction was dealt with as an individual project, hence there were no standard designs. This practice only emerged some 20 years later when the need for boxes to be constructed easily and quickly became evident to meet increasing demands. Even then, site restrictions, size of box required, the use of materials, in some cases to match those of existing buildings, plus the various railway companies' personal preferences, all led to innumerable departures from any standard design.

Consequently, very few of the boxes on the railway network were completely identical in appearance. One thing was constant though. From the gargantuan 250-lever brick-built boxes controlling busy urban locations, right down to the humble wooden signal cabins guarding nothing more than an isolated level crossing hidden deep in the countryside, every signalman had a fierce pride in his work and, especially, in the pristine condition of his box. For example, to avoid any chance of tarnishing the gleaming brass handles, signal and point levers would be pulled only by hands covered with a cloth, and lino floors would be polished to shine like glass. In the more remote locations, where traffic was sparse, and spare time was available, small, neatly planted flowerbeds would often be found nearby too. Progress happens of course but, sadly, the demise of thousands of mechanical signal boxes which seemed to have personalities of their own, together with the semaphore signals they operated, in favour of just a few austere, featureless power boxes controlling coloured lights, has surely resulted in an immense loss to the visual interest of Britain's railway scene.

Bright lights overhead; the glare of large electric lamps outside; the flashing of hand-signals,
red, white and green, on every hand below; the snort of passing engines, their deafening whistles,
far and near, and of every variety; whiffs of nauseous smoke; shouting from
the shunters below; and as a constant accompaniment to all that, the ringing of bells,
the snap and clang, the rattle and wrench of numberless lever handles.

James Scott, 'Railway Romance and other Essays', 1913

BASCHURCH (SHROPSHIRE)

This Mckenzie and Holland Type 3 box stands on the 1848 Chester to Shrewsbury line, which was taken over by the G.W.R in 1854. When in service, the box protected the station area and a level crossing on the B4397, its 25 lever frame dated from 1911. It is now a Grade II listed building as from 1999. The locking room, with arched windows, is of red brick up to operating floor level, with a timber framed and weatherboarded cabin above. The Welsh Slate roof is adorned with one elegant "ball and spearhead" finial, and this end of the box has a timber staircase leading up to a charming porch with a saw-toothed valance over the entrance. Its gabled roof and weatherboarding neatly echoes that of the signal box itself.

Opened 1880   Closed (to passengers) 1960
                     Closed (to freight) 1965

(O.S. Landranger Sht 126   G.R. SJ4222)

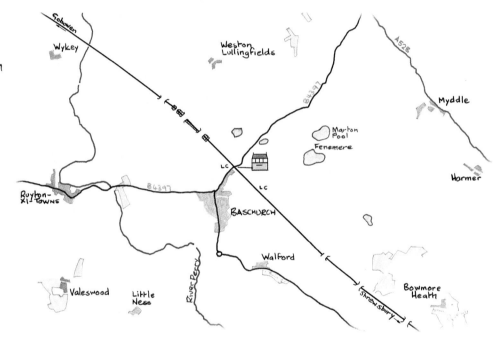

BASCHURCH

13

ADVERSANE (WEST SUSSEX)

This is an example of a "Brighton" style ground level signal box set at a level crossing between Billingshurst and Pulborough. An all timber construction with horizontal boarding, and a pitched, slated roof with large plain bargeboards. The appearance of this rather modest but sturdy structure is greatly enhanced by the addition of a very elegant "Ball and Arrowhead" finial placed at each gabled end of its roof. The use of seriffed lettering on the nameboard is an unusual feature.

This box was demolished sometime before 1977.

(O.S. Landranger Sht 197   G.R. TQ 0723)

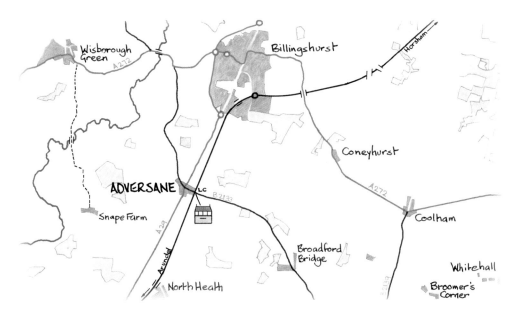

ADVERSANE

The 137-lever frame in Wrawby Junction signal box, North Lincolnshire.

The high house contains many levers, standing in thick, shining ranks. It perfectly resembles an organ in some great church, if it were not that these rows of numbered and indexed handles typify something more acutely human than does a keyboard. It requires four men to play this organ-like thing, and the strains never cease. Night and day, day and night, these four men are walking to and fro, from this lever to that lever, and under their hands the great machine raises its great hymn of a world at work, the fall and rise of signals and the clicking swing of switches.

Stephen Crane, 'The Scotch Express' from 'Men, Women and Boats', 1921

CHANDLERS FORD (HAMPSHIRE)

Chandlers Ford signal box was typical of an early Type1 style adopted by the London and South Western Railway, and was distinctive for its saw-toothed fuscia boards and its unusually large nameboard. The horizontal boarding of the operating floor cabin is a later modification covering previously exposed cross-bracing timbers. A boarded walkway covers pointrodding and signal wires from track to locking room which includes an unusual arched feature in the brickwork.

This box contained a 15 lever Stevens frame.

Opened 1870s   Closed 1969

(O.S. Landranger Sht. 185   G.R. SU4320)

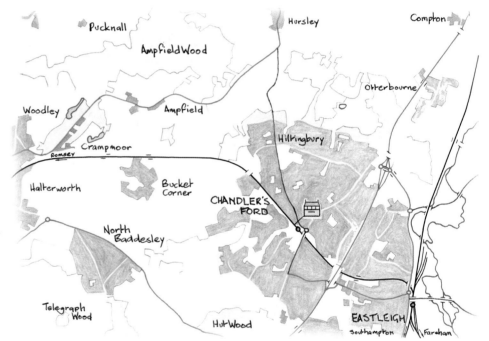

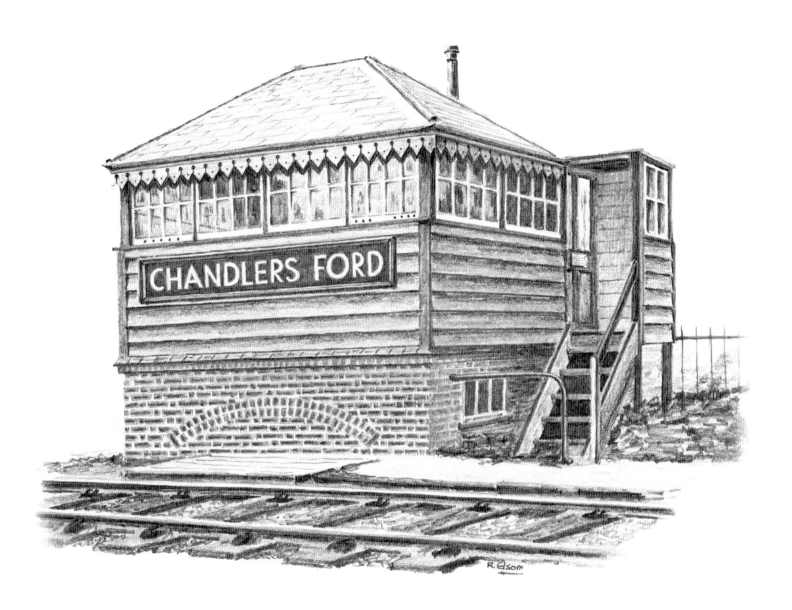

FENCEHOUSES (DURHAM)

The unusual design of this North Eastern signal box, situated 3 miles north of Durham, with its wide all timber cantilevered cabin mounted on a narrow brick base, was necessary because, at one time, four tracks serving the Lambton Colliery route plus sidings passed on both sides of the box. This left little room for a more conventional style of construction.

The diagonal panelling in parts of the timber structure is purely ornamental, and this can be found in some other boxes in this part of the world. Because of the iconic significance of this box, notably, being cantilevered on both sides, it was not originally intended to demolish it after closure. Unfortunately, this became necessary after occupancy by drug users together with serious vandalism.

Opened 1914   Closed 1991

(O.S. Landranger Sht. 88   G.R. NZ 3150)

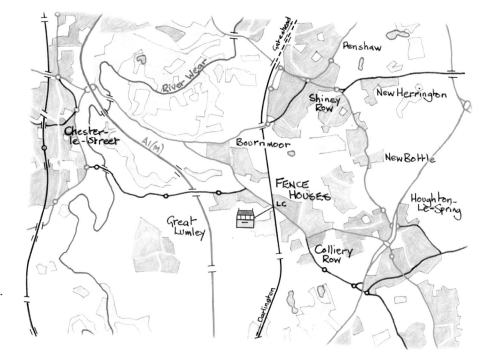

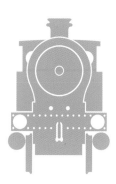

Oft when I feel my engine swerve,
As o'er strange rails we fare,
I strain my eyes around the curve
For what awaits us there.
When swift and free she carries me
Through yards unknown at night,
I look along the line to see
That all the lights are white.

Cy Warman, 'Will the Lights be White?', 1897. From a poem reflecting the trust engine drivers had to have in signalmen, and the early practice of using white lights for the "All Clear".

INVERKEILOR (SCOTLAND)

Inverkeilor signal box was built by the North British Railway to their Type 1 design. A brick based construction up to operating floor level, where windows of 2x2 panes are fixed except for vertical sashes at each end of the front elevation. The usually panelled boards above the windows appear here to have been replaced with horizontal boarding. Also, the lack of fascia boards to the exposed roof rafter ends at the eaves is mystifying, but the slated, hipped roof does conform to standard practice.

This box, still in use, is situated mid way between Arbroath and Montrose on the line from Dundee to Aberdeen.

Its original 16 lever Stevens frame has been extended to 22 levers.

Opened 1881

(O.S. Landranger Sht. 54   G.R. NO6649)

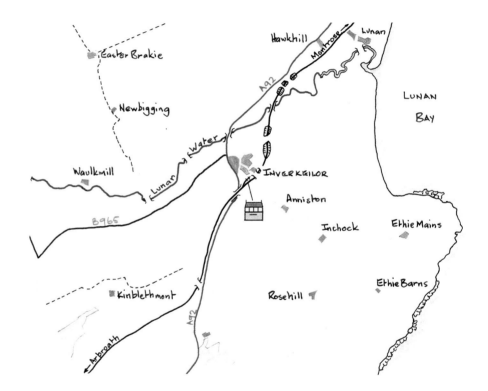

INVERKEILOR

LAUNCESTON (CORNWALL)

Originally built in 1886 as a standard LSWR Type 3 box with an 18 lever frame to control the Southern line from Tavistock. As a cash saving measure the box was enlarged in 1915 to accommodate a second 16 lever frame taken from a signal box controlling the nearby GWR station, thus enabling one signalman to control both stations from one box.

This box lasted until October 1966.

(O.S. Landranger Sht 201   G.R. SX 3285)

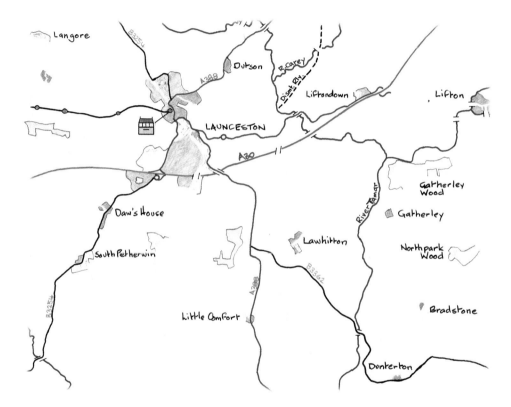

LAUNCESTON

R.Elsom

Photo: Author's Collection

An example of a 'Knee Frame' that I photographed at Tulloch station, Glen Spean, Scotland.
This one unboxed below the quadrant plates and exposed to the elements.

Conventional signal boxes consist generally of two separate sections, a ground-level enclosure to house the locking gear, surmounted by another part containing, amongst a multitude of other things, the lever frame. The problem with the single-storey, ground-level box is how to protect the locking mechanism from all the activity going on above at the lever frame. To resolve this, the Stevens and Sons Company designed a special lever frame for ground-level boxes. The quadrant plates, i.e. the curved, slotted plates through which the levers travel when pushed and pulled to operate the signals etc., were located halfway up the levers, and the area below the quadrant plates was boxed in to protect the locking gear. The presence of this raised portion over the locking gear gave this type of frame the name 'knee frame', probably because the signalman kept striking his knees on the raised quadrant plates when operating the levers. The name has become so commonly used that these frames are rarely referred to as anything else!

BRAUNTON GATES (DEVON)

Used only as a ground frame, Braunton Gates box was constructed partly from second hand materials. When the Ilfracombe line was doubled in 1889, Braunton station received a new box, and the roof timbers and windows of the existing station box were used here at Braunton Gates, the recycled materials being erected on top of a new cement rendered brick base. Not being entirely purpose built, this box was much bigger than it needed to be. Its size could easily have accommodated a frame of at least 16 levers, but all it contained was a small "knee" frame of 5 levers, three of which were spare anyway. The box remained in use until closure of the line in October 1970, thus serving for a total of 91 years.

Opened 1889   Closed 1970
(O.S. Landranger Sht. 180   G.R. SS486364)

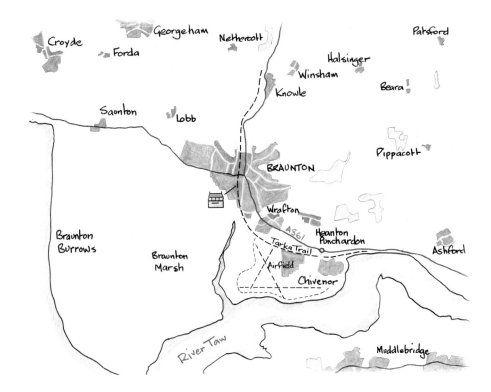

ACHNASHEEN (SCOTLAND)

Achnasheen is on the branch line from Dingwall to Kyle of Lochalsh and, like most Highland Railway stations, had two signal boxes, one at each end of a passing loop. This box is Achnasheen West, identifiable by the roof finials (these were missing on the East box), and was near the station platform controlling the station area, plus the west end of a lengthy passing loop. It was built to McKenzie and Holland's design, but with features peculiar to the Highland Railway such as the battened vertical boarding. The box contained a 16 lever frame. Neither box was manned conventionally, but were worked more like ground frames because the signalling instruments were in the Booking Office, and the signalman would only visit the boxes to set the passing loop points and clear the signals. Probably not much fun on a raw Scottish winter's day!

Opened 1894   Closed 1984
(O.S. Landranger Sht. 25   G.R. NH 1658)

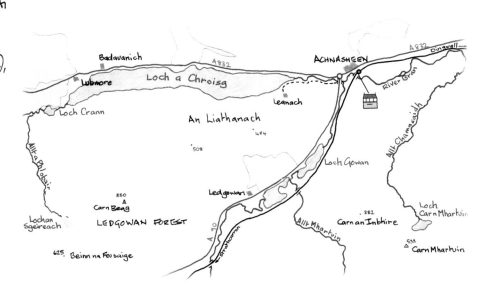

I met this signalman on a trip around Sussex in 1985, in his box at Southbourne station level crossing. A friendly soul, he immediately invited me up and showed me around his domain, of which he was obviously so proud.

The signalman in charge of the traffic should be placed so that he can easily be approached or spoken to by the station-master, or other authorised persons; but it should be rendered difficult for anyone to go into the signal cabin, except in open view, and the cabin should be glazed all round, so that not only can the signalman see outwards, but the station-master can see inwards, and detect any gossiping or idling.

John Wolfe Barry, 'Railway Apprentice', 1887

KNIGHTS HILL SIDINGS (GREATER LONDON)

A small 'Brighton' style signal box of all-timber construction with a noteworthy metal ventilator cum finial on the roof. Positioned just north of Tulse Hill on the South Bermondsey to Leatherhead line. It served a goods siding for the London North Western Railway until 1956 when the siding became a coal depot. This finally closed in October 1968. (O.S. Landranger Sht 176   G.R. TQ 3273)

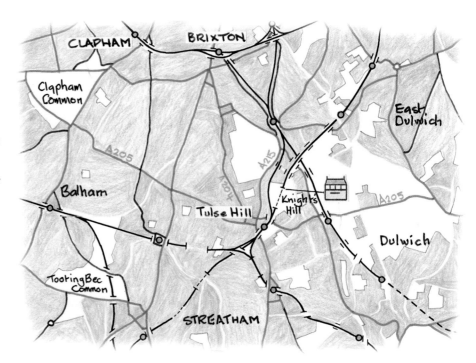

KNIGHTS HILL SIDINGS

R. Elsom

BEALINGS (SUFFOLK)

Everything about this Great Eastern signal box illustrates the immense amount of care and attention given to its design, and it is a long way from the simple huts that were provided for the "policemen" of the early days of railway signalling. Architectural enrichments abound here, from the elegantly "crowned" chimney pot right down to the crenellated brick panels into which the locking room windows are set. In between, the operating floor cabin is distinctively glazed with exceptionally slender glazing bars to windows, and unusual four-paned upper lights. Panelled eaves boards are also a rare feature. The verandah, giving access to the windows for cleaning, is fully covered by the wide overhanging roof, which is itself embellished with decorative ridge tiles, valancing, and barge boards.

This stylish Saxby+Farmer box, containing an 18 lever frame, was situated at a level crossing 76 miles from London between Ipswich and Lowestoft. To construct, the box cost £403.17s.1d. and lasted a cool 100 years. Pretty good value for money methinks!

Opened 1884   Closed 1984

(O.S. Landranger Sht. 169   G.R. TM 2347)

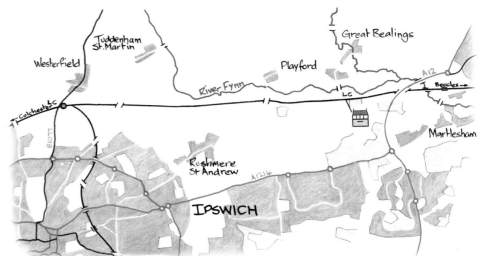

So, having bought the signalman, according to design,
They simply went and placed him in a box beside the line,
And shirked responsibility and worry's weighty load,
By not so much as teaching him a word about the "code".
They told him to amuse himself, the box was pretty full
Of bells for him to play upon, and levers he could pull;
They never told him which of them was right, and which was wrong
But left him and forgot him. Then they sent the trains along.

Excerpt from the poem 'The Neglected Signalman', Fun, Vol. 35, 1882

BINEGAR (SOMERSET)

Sited on the 'up' platform, Binegar signal box is typical of Somerset and Dorset railway construction, with its railway brick and timber superstructure on a local limestone base. The box's decorative bargeboards being repeated on the adjoining waiting shelter. A double-ended finial completes the ornamentation. This box lay on the Somerset and Dorset line between Radstock and Shepton Mallet, and it contained a Saxby and Farmer frame of 22 levers. Binegar was a very busy box, and one incident there resulted in a fatality that clearly illustrates the importance of any signalman's job.

In July 1885, the signalman diverted an up express which collided with a goods train standing on the down line, resulting in one death and seven injuries. At the time, alterations were being made to the interlocking gear in the signal box, but the signalman had not been fully instructed, and he pulled the wrong lever. He was tried for manslaughter but, as the accident was not entirely his fault, he was acquitted.

Opened 1885   Closed 1966

(O.S. Landranger   Sht. 183   G.R. ST6149)

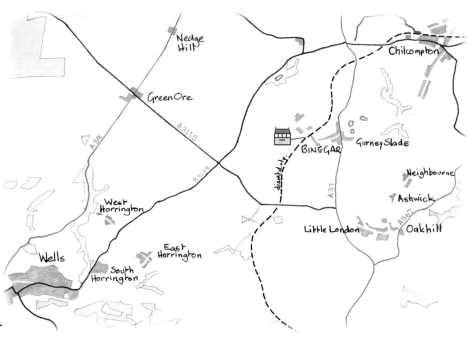

BINEGAR

R.Elsom

The station is a quiet one but suits me, sir" he said,
I once was signal man, you see, and now that job I dread.
You see that box just over there? 'Tis where we switch fast trains,
From side tracks to the centre rails, it takes good nerve and brains;
For if you're too late at the switch, a second, naught can check,
A terrible collision, which means awful death and wreck!
Oh, sometimes when I'd think of this 'twould drive me nearly wild.
As each night in our little home I'd kiss my wife and child.

Wm. H. Friday, 'The Story of the Signalman', a song from 1896

This was what the pointsman said,
With both hands at his throbbing head –
"I drew the wrong lever standing here
And the danger signals stood at clear,
But before I could draw it back again
On came the fast express, and then –
There came a roar and a crash that shook
This cabin floor, but I could not look
At the wreck, for I knew the dead would peer
With strange dull eyes at their murderer here.

Alexander Anderson, from the poem 'Drew the Wrong Lever', 1880

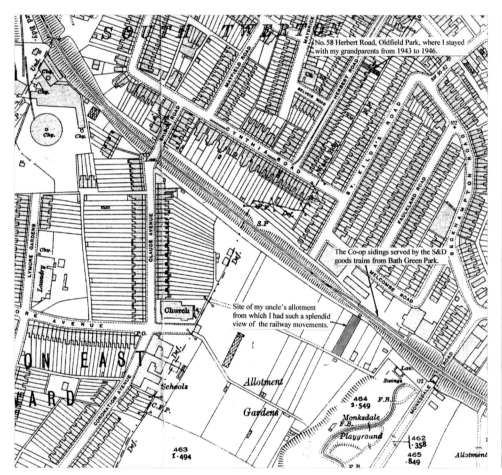

No. 58 Herbert Road, Oldfield Park, where I stayed with my grandparents from 1943 to 1946.

The Co-op sidings served by the S&D goods trains from Bath Green Park.

Site of my uncle's allotment from which I had such a splendid view of the railway movements.

Above left: Ordnance Survey County Series 1/2500 Sht, XIV.5, 1930, showing locations of where I was living in the 1940s, and my view of the railway.
My friends and I were frequent visitors to the nearby Monksdale playground too, where we could sail our model boats on the very shallow stream running through it.

Above right: A Somerset & Dorset 7F No. 53800 and its banker storm up the 1 in 50 bank out of Bath, bound for Evercreech Junction, with the rows of terraced housing of Oldfield Park in the background. This magnificent sight is the kind of thing I was often unwittingly privileged to see as a ten-year-old in 1945, and is virtually the same viewpoint I had from the bottom of my uncle's garden.

Although I never visited the station at Binegar when it was operating, it does have a special meaning for me, simply because my Grandfather (on my mother's side) was employed by the Somerset & Dorset Railway for many years. I'm not exactly sure what his full job description was, but one of his tasks was to check the rolling stock wheels for damage by striking each one with a long-handled hammer; the resulting note produced would tell him if the wheel was in good order or not. This he would do at Bath Green Park station, the northern terminus of the S&D. During World War 2, at the age of eight, I was evacuated from Bristol and stayed with him where he lived in Oldfield Park, Bath. He was retired then, but still possessed his railwayman's pocket-watch on a heavy chain which he wore in his waistcoat pocket. One of my endearing memories of him is his daily routine of ceremoniously, and with great reverence, slowly withdrawing the watch from his pocket to ensure that the house clock on the mantelpiece was correct.

It was never the other way round, that watch was always the timepiece to trust, it was never wrong. I could imagine him doing just that on the platform of Green Park station, checking the train movements in and out. Also during my stay at Oldfield Park (1943-46) I would spend many a happy hour with my uncle on his allotment which lay alongside the S&D line directly opposite the Co-Op siding which the rail traffic served with coal and bakery products (see the map opposite). Somerset & Dorset traffic travelling south from Bath Green Park terminus would be diverted from the main Bristol to Bath GWR line on to the S&D line by the Bath Junction signal box. This stretch of the line from Bath to Combe Down tunnel, which passed the end of my uncle's allotment, was a grinding 1 in 50 gradient. I can still remember the sight and especially the sounds of many a 7F locomotive, together with its banking engine, pounding up that incline in clouds of billowing steam. Such contented days for me, despite the horrors of that war.

Roger Elsom
Southampton 2023

bought this cast iron Somerset and Dorset sign at one of
the annual Auto Jumbles held at Beaulieu in Hampshire.
It is, I think, a winsomely innocent, nostalgic piece of British
railway history, raising, as it does, a smile, with its somewhat
risqué warning. It also says so much about the differences between
19th century culture and standards, compared with those of today.

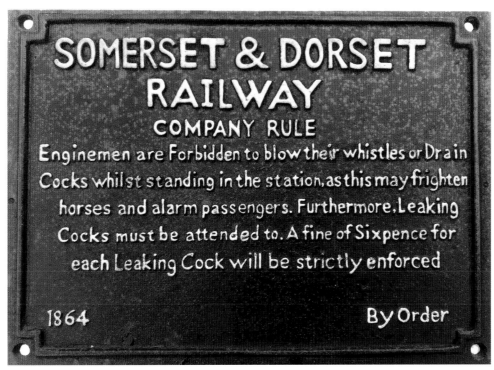

SWADLINCOTE JUNCTION (DERBYSHIRE)

Unless site constraints dictated otherwise, most Midland Railway signal boxes were built from standard prefabricated parts. Standard panels came in 10', 12', and 15' lengths and could be used in any combination to suit the size of box required. All timber construction and hipped roofs remained as constant features. This Midland box, a Type 4d, consists of two 10' x 10' cabins "stitched" together. The absence of the usual "Ball + Arrowhead" finials which graced the roofs of many such boxes suggests it was probably built after the 1st World War when lack of materials, labour, and money saw the end of such refinements for quite some time.

Opened probably post 1918   Closed 1969
(O.S. Landranger Sht 128   G.R. SK 2916)

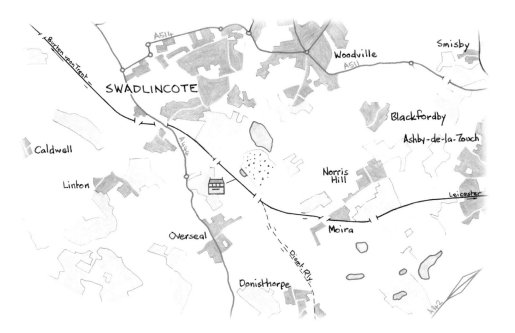

CORFE CASTLE (DORSET)

This image is of the original London and South Western Railway wooden structure with a hipped roof. It contained a 32 lever frame, and was set on the down platform. Bizarrely, the front facing windows have been boarded over. This was done purely to preserve the modesty of the station master's wife whose bedroom it overlooked. Had she never heard of curtains? The signalman's sight lines must surely have been compromised by this arrangement! The line this box stood on between Swanage and the main line at Wareham was closed by British Rail and ripped up in seven weeks in 1972. Thanks largely to the resolve of volunteers who rebuilt part of the line between Swanage and Norden and ran it as a tourist attraction, Swanage was finally reconnected to Wareham in June 2017, and this box has now been rebuilt to resemble the original. Costing £48,000, it took four years to complete and now, significantly, has a fully glazed front!

Opened 1885 Closed 1956

(O.S. Landranger Sht 195 G.R. SY 9682)

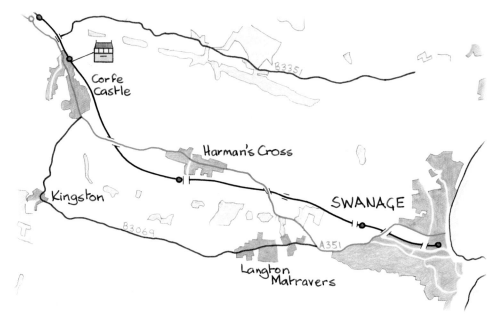

"Beige Marks and Spencer anorak, elasticated
cuffs, fully enclosable hood...I don't believe
I've got that one."

If you can sit for hours on draughty stations
With Job-like patience till the trains go through;
If you can put behind you all temptations,
To cross the line and get a "better view";
If you can wait and not get tired by waiting,
Or, being shouted at, not answer back,
Or being hated, not give way to hating,
And slyly try to "trespass on the track"
If you can brave the righteous wrath of porters,
And still observe the rulings of the game;
If you can take a hand with those "defaulters",
And keep your schoolboy honour just the same;
If you can fill each unforgiving minute
With sixty seconds' worth of "Spotting" done,
Yours is the world and everything that's in it,
And what is more, you'll be a "Spotter", son.

Margaret Brannigan (former secretary to Ian Allan;
with her apologies to Kipling), Trains Illustrated No. 4, 1947

CLACHNAHARRY (SCOTLAND)

This McKenzie and Holland Type 3 box conforms to Highland Railway design with its vertical boarding to all sides. The box stands at a fairly rare example of a single line token station that has no passing loops or sidings. Since the singling of the double track westwards to Clunes in 1966, Clachnaharry has only controlled the swing-bridge over the northern end of the Caledonian Canal, together with its protecting signals. This it does with just 4 levers. A notable feature here is the inclusion of the two fine, slender 'Ball and Spear' finials on the roof. These do much to enhance the appearance of this already very tidy looking structure.

Opened 1912

(O.S. Landranger Sht. 26   G.R. NH 6546)

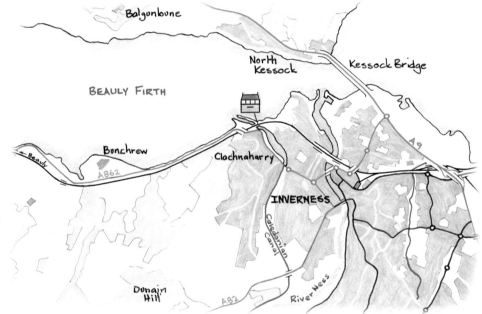

56

DRIGG (CUMBRIA)

One of the oldest Furness Railway boxes, and displays the early stone-to-operating floor construction typical of these Type1 buildings. The base blends random rubble with dressed stone at the corners, finished at the operating floor level with a course of splayed stones. The upper, slightly smaller, cabin consists of a substantial timber frame, horizontal boarding, and windows with no horizontal glazing bars, thus emphasising the vertical nature of the box. Narrow upper lights lead to a hipped roof, a common feature of all Furness boxes. This box also includes the unusual practice, adopted by the L.M.S. on its Furness section, of placing the nameboard above eaves level. Drigg box is located on the Cumbrian coastal route between Ravenglass and Seascale, and controls a minor road and station level crossing with its Railway Signal Company 13 lever frame.

When I visited Drigg in 1987, I was unaware that this seemingly innocent and peaceful part of England was implicated in a contentious matter. During World War 2, a Royal Ordnance Factory was established at Drigg between the railway and the sea, and is now the site of a nuclear low-level radio active waste repository. As the area is vulnerable to flooding which might cause the waste to leak onto the shoreline, local residents are naturally concerned.

Opened   Early 1870s

(O.S. Landranger Sht. 96   G.R. SD 0698)

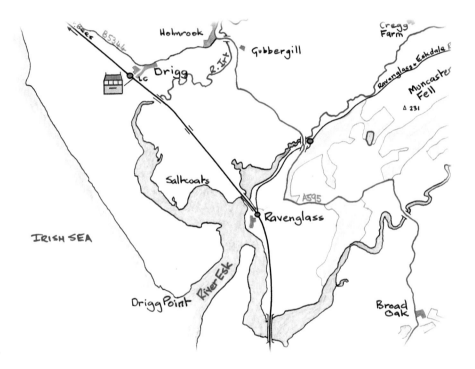

The smell of well-buffed lino; the sight of brightly coloured levers, polished wooden block instruments, gleaming brass-work; the sound of bells pinging, levers crashing and gates clattering; Victoriana alive and well and still earning its keep.

As a 10-year-old, signalman John Illingworth recalls visiting his first signal box.
From 'Resignalling Britain' by Michael Rhodes, 2015

Photo: Kevin Robertson

Idyllic summer days with the windows and doors open, the ping of the bells floating across the surrounding countryside, birds tweeting. Compare and contrast with the dark winter nights, rain beating like shot on the windows of your cosy little box as a distant twinkling blue white light is observed steadily growing in size until a train emerges, rippled through water-dimpled windows, only to recede into the distance as a diminishing red tail-light.

More reminiscences of signalman John Illingworth, also from 'Resignalling Britain'

GLENWHILLY (DUMFRIES + GALLOWAY)

This is one of the earliest examples of a Glasgow + South Western Type 7 signal box, which contained a Stevens 20 lever frame at the back, and a stove-pipe at the front of the cabin. Improved visibility is given by the deeper than usual operating floor windows. The locking room windows, three panes high, are usual for the period. Glenwhilly is situated at a passing loop on the single line between Ayr and Stranraer Harbour. This box works to Barrhill box 6 miles to the north, and to Dunragit box 10 miles to the south. Opened 1905
(. O.S. Landranger Sht. 76   G.R. NX 1771)

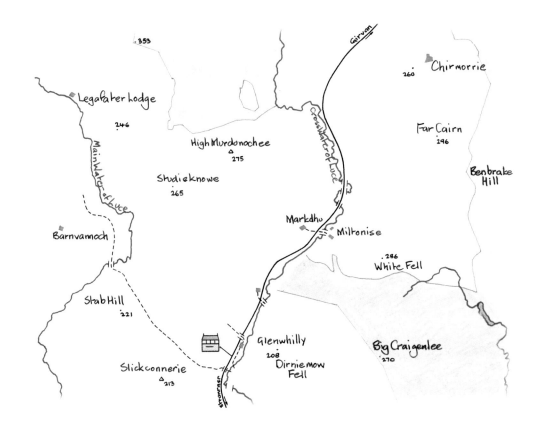

.353

Girvan

Chirmorrie
260

Legafater Lodge

Crosswater of Luce

Far Cairn
296

246

High Murdonochee
△ 275

Benbrake Hill

Main Water of Luce

Studieknowe
265

Markdhu

Miltonise

Barnvamoch

.286
White Fell

StabHill
221

Glenwhilly
208

Big Craigenlee
.270

Slickconnerie
△ 213

Dirniemow Fell

Stranraer

62

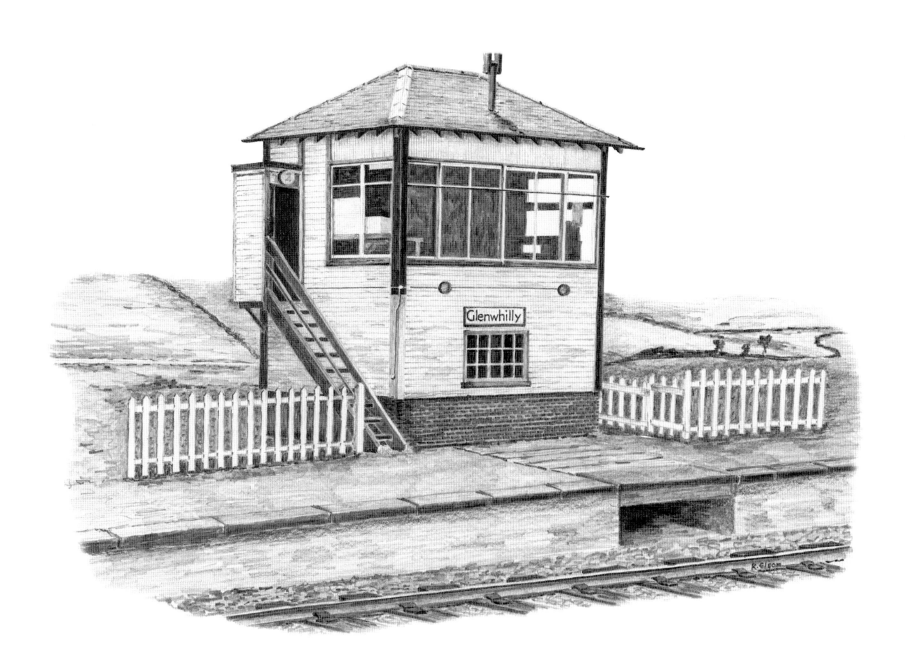

WOODGATE (WEST SUSSEX)

Situated four miles east of Chichester, this Saxby and Farmer signal cabin controlled a level crossing on the A29 to Bognor Regis. This is a neatly proportioned structure with its Flemish Bond brickwork, deep windows topped by upper lights, and slender wooden eaves brackets supporting the overhanging slated, hipped roof. A sizeable brick chimney for this relatively small building completes the picture. My primary reason for including this box in my collection of drawings is because of its simple charm. Unfortunately, despite some exhaustive research, I have not been able to establish exactly when it was built or demolished.

(O.S. Landranger Sht.197   G.R. SU9304)

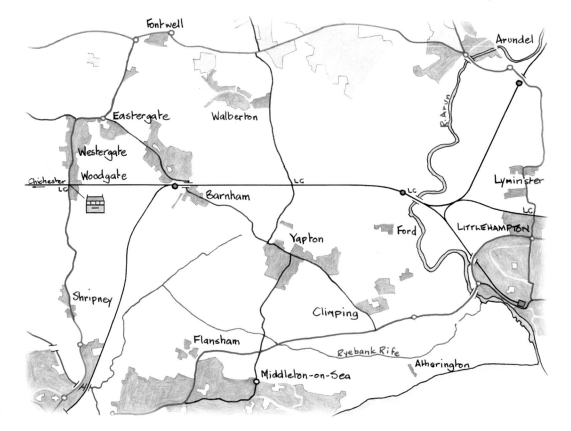

WOODGATE

It was also during the night turn that we were visited by our nocturnal residents, the rats. These pests used to scurry along the back of the lever frame in their constant foraging for food, having found their way into the box through the numerous slots and holes necessary at ground level for the operating rods and wires. A specially balanced and sharpened poker was kept to throw at these rats in the hope that one day we would kill one and so frighten the others away. In the time I was in the box I witnessed hundreds of vain attempts to achieve the impossible for I never saw one hit – never mind killed. I don't know why we bothered, because the railway employed an official rat-catcher.

M. Burke, 'Signalman' 1982

HOLMSLEY (HAMPSHIRE)

Basically, a Type I LSWR box, but the addition of the roof vent classifies this one as a Type IA. Why so much extra ventilation was thought to be necessary on such a small building already supplied with opening windows is a bit of a mystery. Always a source of annoying draughts, the signalmen often inserted rags etc. around it thus making its intended purpose superfluous anyway. The design, never widely used, did survive in a few places until the 1960s.

Holmsley box remained active until the Ringwood line was closed in May 1964.

It contained a 13 lever Stevens frame.

(O.S. Landranger Sht 195 G.R. SU231006)

PARK SOUTH (CUMBRIA)

Originally 'Thwaite Flat Junction', but was renamed in 1882. Park South is so named because there was a Park North box controlling a level crossing 858 yards away. This is one of only two Furness Type 3 boxes surviving (the other being at St Bees), and it lies at the north east corner of its level crossing on the Cumbrian coast line controlling a minor road/rail crossing plus the Dalton loop junction 1km to the south. The tapered walls of Park South's stone-to-floor base is an instantly recognisable Type 3 feature, the stonework here being unusually regular. Other typical features are the sub-divided upper lights of the operating floor windows, the inclusion of some wooden shutters, and the steeply pitched hipped roof. Arched locking room windows complete the scene. The box contains a 24 lever frame supplied by The Railway Signal Company.

Opened 1883

(O.S. Landranger Sht. 96   G.R. SD 2174)

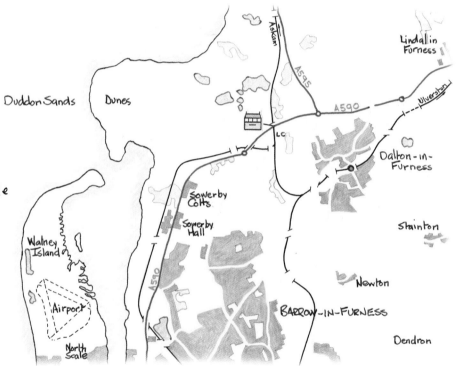

Letter from the Stationmaster at Pembrey & Burry Port
to Inspector Pullen at Carmarthen on 15th May, 1943:

Since your Department attended to the working of the points lever at
Dock Junction Box this week, an improvement has certainly been effected,
which makes it much easier for the lever to be pushed back in the frame.
The pulling portion is, however, about the same as it was before, and
although Miss Melton can manage it fairly well, Miss Morgans, who is slightly
built, has a little difficulty in doing so. I have no doubt that, with a little
practice, she could master this, but if something further can be done to
ease the pulling operation, it would be a distinct advantage.

Steve Daly, "Signalwomen", signalbox.org

From the beginning, male dominance on British railways prevailed. It was reinforced by the wearing of military style uniforms, a rigidly adhered to pecking order of rank, together with stringent codes of discipline. All very reminiscent of the armed forces in fact. Before 1915 when women actually achieved some level of equality by gaining union membership, they were almost exclusively excluded from any kind of employment on the railways. There was no doubt about the simple fact – that railway work was men's work, and that was that, according to the men!

There was some female involvement before that, however. From around the 1830s, women could be found in a few low-grade positions, but with absolutely no hope of future promotion; until 1914 that is, when the First World War saw a third of the male workers joining the forces. Suddenly, the value of women in railway jobs that had been so rigidly closed to them was realised. But still, incredibly, despite this obvious answer to the nation's desperate need for those jobs to be filled quickly, there was still strong opposition to their inclusion, and Union leaders insisted they be dismissed immediately after the war.

It's almost unbelievable, and difficult to understand why Union opposition was so fierce then. When a few females were recruited as signalwomen for example, railwaymen tried to prevent them from being trained, and threatened to strike. The men, amazingly, declared that women lacked sufficient common sense and intelligence required to carry out the work properly. How appalling is that totally misguided kind of thinking? In fact, female guards and signallers proved, in the end, to be completely competent, as they did in other aspects of the railway industry they were involved in.

At the conclusion of the war in 1918, there were over 60,000 women employed in virtually all types of work, even in jobs previously considered beyond them such as the operation of marshalling yard points, and many other heavy engineering tasks. There was no sensible reason why those same female workers should not have stayed on after 1918, but by 1923 their numbers had been drastically reduced to under 200, and by the mid-1920s women were once again restricted to poorly paid menial tasks.

Things did improve considerably between the two World Wars, and at the start of the Second World War some 25,000 women were working on the railways, but they were still engaged mainly in routine jobs like catering, cleaning and office work. When thousands of railway men left to join the forces in 1939, once again, surprise surprise, women were deemed capable of carrying out so-called "men's" work. Disturbingly, however, there was a repeat of the bitter opposition as more and more women took on crucial jobs to keep the trains running. Significantly, many became signal women, and were allowed to work the more complicated signal boxes which previously had been denied them due to their allegedly suspect mental and physical capabilities. The concern about their physical ability was at least a potentially relevant one, as it could take a considerable amount of strength to pull off a signal arm situated a long way from the box. (The furthest distance from signal to box was, to my knowledge, the Hertford North Up Distant, some 2,367 yards away.) As for the concerns about signalwomen's mental capacity, that just beggars belief!

There seemed to be so much comment about the ability of women to do what had always been considered exclusively a man's job. Railway magazines at the time implored passengers to limit the weight of their luggage and parcels because "the women are willing, but even a willing horse can be overloaded". Another reporter patronisingly explained, "This plea is based on gallantry to those of the weaker sex".

It is at least good to know that, at the same time these so ill-informed journalists, sat in the comfort of their workplaces, were writing things like this, the so-called 'weaker sex' was out there, engaged in most, if not all, aspects of the railway business, just getting on with what had to be done, many of them carrying out their duties in all weathers.

Mrs. Kathleen Willingham, 36 years old and married with children, worked from 9am until 10.30pm, a 91-hour week, at a level crossing near Colchester. She had to pull a heavy lever 144 times a day. The LNER provided a stand-in for only seven hours a week "shopping leave". Her application for a pay-rise to compensate for taking over her husband's duties was declined. She asked to get her hours reduced but the LNER treated her as a part-time employee because she could "run home between trains".

Helena Wojtczak, 'Railway Women', 2005

DUNBRIDGE (HAMPSHIRE)

Situated between Romsey and Salisbury, this was not so much a signal box — more, a converted cottage. Here, the original cottage still stands under and around the box, with the locking gear located in what was once the sitting room. The date of its conversion is unknown, but the superstructure is very like the standard design of the 1880s, with its horizontal weather-boarding. The retained brick chimney and distinctive 'torpedo' roof vent was however unusual. This box enjoyed a long life of 100 years or more, and originally contained a gate wheel together with a Stevens 18 lever frame, later increased to 21.

Opened around 1875   Closed 1983
(O.S. Landranger Sht. 185   G.R. SU 3126)

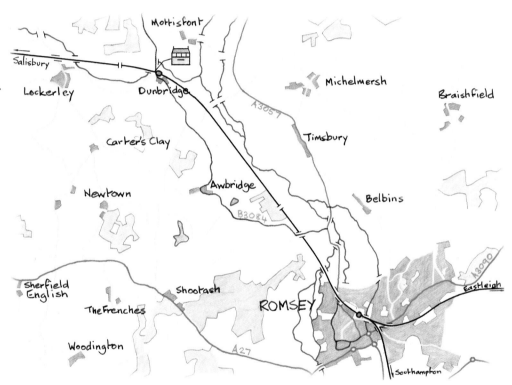

76

MEDGE HALL (SOUTH YORKSHIRE)

This gate box, built by the Railway Signal Company for the Manchester, Sheffield and Lincolnshire Railway, stands on the north side of a level crossing on the line between Doncaster and Scunthorpe. Containing a Railway Signal Company 7 lever frame, it enjoys a quiet, rural location alongside the Sheffield and South Yorkshire Navigation. Boaters on the canal are unable to operate the nearby Crook 'O Moor Swing Bridge until the crossing keeper at Medge Hall box has closed the gates on the adjacent railway.
Opened 1886   Closed probably in 2013
(O.S. Landranger Sht. 112   G.R. SE 7412)

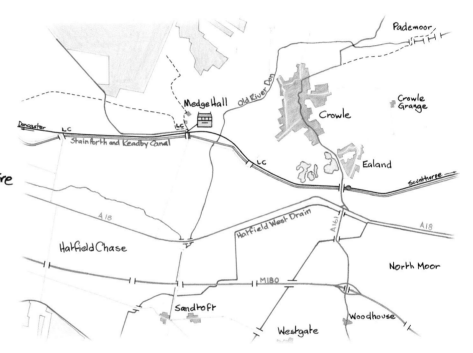

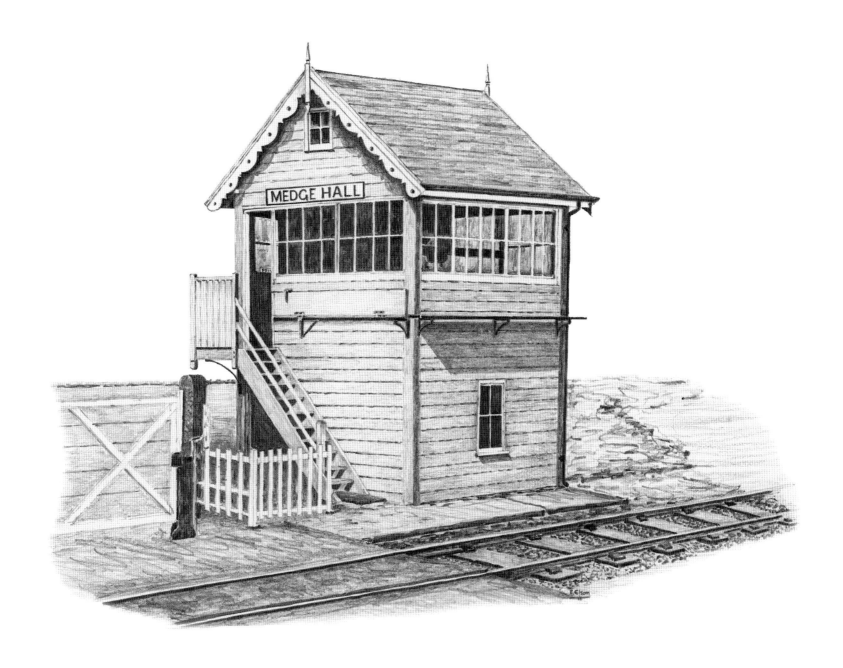

MEDGE HALL

Medge Hall Signal Box, Doncaster, 1988

This photo was taken during our tour of Humberside. We were a bit disappointed not to be invited up to visit his box, but this signalman was extremely friendly, and very interested in why we were there, and amazed that we had travelled all the way from Southampton just to photograph the signal boxes in the area.

Avonmouth Dock Junction Signal Box, Bristol, 1988

This friendly signalman invited us into his box, simply because, he admitted, he was a
bit bored as that Sunday's rail traffic was quite light, and he was glad of someone to
talk to. Here he is pulling off a signal just for our benefit and our cameras, although
no train was due. Unfortunately, he didn't suggest that we might have a go ourselves,
which was probably, quite rightly, a step too far for him to risk!

NORTH WALSHAM (NORFOLK)

A standard all timber Great Eastern signal box, fitted with a 'look out' extension at one end to provide greater visibility for the signal man. It was mounted on the down side platform on the line between Norwich and Cromer. This box was originally known as North Walsham Station as there was another box nearby controlling a junction, but it became plain North Walsham when the junction box closed in 1956. It was fitted with a McKenzie and Holland 31 lever frame.

Opened 1896   Closed 2000

(O.S. Landranger Sht. 133   G.R. TG 2829)

Torrington (Devon)

Opened in 1872 when the line from Ilfracombe to Bideford was extended to Torrington, this box displays some individualistic features. From ground to operating floor level the materials used are a mixture of brick and rubble masonry. The large, dressed stone blocks forming the quoins do display some kind of symmetry, but the random manner in which the rest of the materials of the base of this box have been put together ensures at least that no other signal box will ever look exactly like this one, even if similar materials are used. The box closed in September 1970.

Opened 1872   Closed 1970

(O.S. Landranger Sht. 180   G.R. ss 480198)

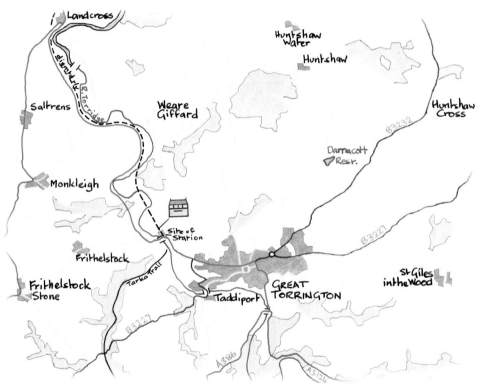

The Daily Mail reported, in February 2013, that many frustrated passengers were held up for a whole hour when a signalman got stuck in the toilet. The copy read: 'The worker had dashed from his post to the nearby Victorian outhouse to answer the call of nature, but the embarrassed signalman had to be freed by colleagues when the lock became stuck. His cries for help were eventually heard coming from the brick toilet at the manned signal box at Henwick, Worcestershire.' Publicly, rail management announced that the delay was caused by "signalling problems". One website user, who obviously somehow had knowledge of the real reason, quipped, "Where are the relief staff when you need them?"

Despite the immense amount of responsibility that signalmen held in carrying out their duties, I can imagine that working in a signal box must have been generally enjoyable. Those employed in major station and junction boxes always had plenty to think about, of course, but even those working alone at isolated rural level crossing locations, with perhaps few rail movements to control, could still communicate with their colleagues in other boxes through their telephones and telegraph systems. Wherever they worked they all had the means to make a brew whenever they wished and could always keep warm in the coldest of winters by stoking up their trusty stoves. The signal wires, however, were always exposed to the elements and were therefore likely to corrode in time. They were well galvanized and regularly checked for any weaknesses, but any powerful pull on the lever in the box could still cause the signalman problems. If a signal wire did break when the signalman pulled a lever he could end up anywhere but where he should be in the signal box and obviously, if unlucky, suffer some considerable physical damage. It has been known, apparently, for some poor unfortunates to end up on top of their red-hot stoves!

HORSEMOOR (CAMBRIDGESHIRE)

Situated two miles south east of March on the Ely to Peterborough line, this box controlled a level crossing on the B1099. Built entirely of timber with horizontal boarding to both locking room and operating floor sections, it had a slate roof that extended fully over the entrance balcony. This at least afforded a certain amount of protection from the elements. The box escaped demolition after its closure and has, apparently, been relocated alongside another dismantled railway line near the village of Murrow in Cambridgeshire.

Opened 1899   Closed 1988

(O.S. Landranger   Sht. 143   G.R. TL 4396)

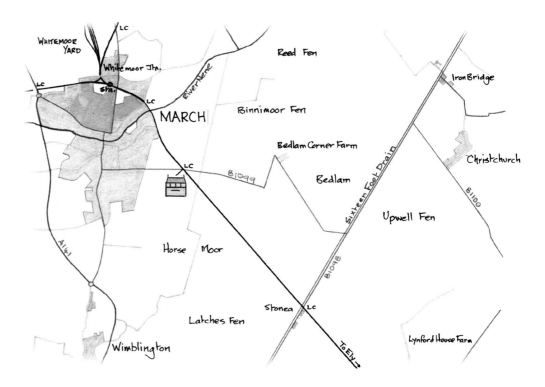

HORSEMOOR

R. Elsom

SALISBURY TUNNEL JUNCTION (WILTSHIRE)

Typical of the earliest boxes of the South Western Railway, this one at Salisbury is mostly constructed of brick, but with less window area than that found in later structures. It also has a gabled roof – others had hipped roofs. The interior of this box is so small that the 21 lever frame and booking desk occupied most of the space, so the sink and signalman's locker were housed in the porch. The box was located in a deep cutting east of Salisbury station at the end of a tunnel where the line from Eastleigh and Southampton joined the Waterloo line.

Opened 1870   Closed 1981
(O.S. Landranger   Sht. 184   G.R. SU1430)

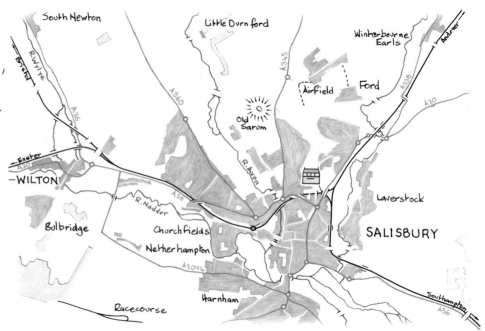

The signalman's view of Salisbury Tunnel's east portal.

A signalman's outlook from his signal box could be hugely varied according to where his box was sited. In busy station locations, at least there would be the everyday human activity around him to provide some interest. The solitude of the rural signalman could be relieved by befriending some of the local people who passed his box regularly and he might well enjoy splendid, uplifting views too. But let's spare a thought for the less fortunate individual who had to work in a box set deep in a cutting somewhere, with nothing much to see apart from blank wall or banks rising just a few metres from his windows, with just a narrow ribbon of sky high above him. By the very nature of the terrain, tunnels were also often to be found in cuttings, and their dark, chilling portals only added to the somewhat eerie surroundings. Salisbury Tunnel Junction box was in just such a location, maybe not in as deep a cutting as some, but deep enough nevertheless, and was probably not one eagerly sought after by signalmen. Charles Dickens must have had similar thoughts about this because, in 1866, he wrote quite a long ghost story about a signalman working in this kind of setting, and he captures in his own inimitable way the nature of the aura that prevailed in such places.

SIDMOUTH (DEVON)

Constructed when the Sidmouth branch line opened in 1874, this London and South Western Railway Type 1 box is taller than usual for the type. It also displays here an addition of perhaps the smallest extension ever made to a signal box, with just a couple of feet being added to the operating floor cabin, cantilevered out from one end. When and why this was done is not known. Shiplap boarding to the upper floor enclosure is capped with a slated, hipped roof, and the whole surmounts quite a lofty locking room. This latter is brick built in Flemish Bond ie. alternate headers and stretchers in each course of the wall faces. Sidmouth box contained a 23 lever Stevens frame, and it lasted until the closure of the line to all traffic in May 1967.

Opened 1874   Closed 1967
(O.S.Landranger Sht. 192   G.R. SY121885)

R. Elson

MEATHOP (CUMBRIA)

A Furness Type 2 signal box showing the company's stone-to-floor style of construction common until the late 1890s. Type 2 boxes shared several common features despite the lack of overall standardisation, notably, the absence of fascia boards, the provision of inside boarding only for the operating floor walls (hence the exposed cross members seen here), and windows with no horizontal glazing bars. As here, there was often a boarded section in the centre of the box front elevation. All Furness boxes had hipped roofs and, like other Cumbrian boxes, usually echoed the style and materials of nearby station buildings. Meathop was approximately 1¼ miles from Grange over Sands to the west, and 1¾ miles from Arnside to the east.
Opened circa 1879
(O.S. Landranger Sht. 97   G.R. SD 4779)

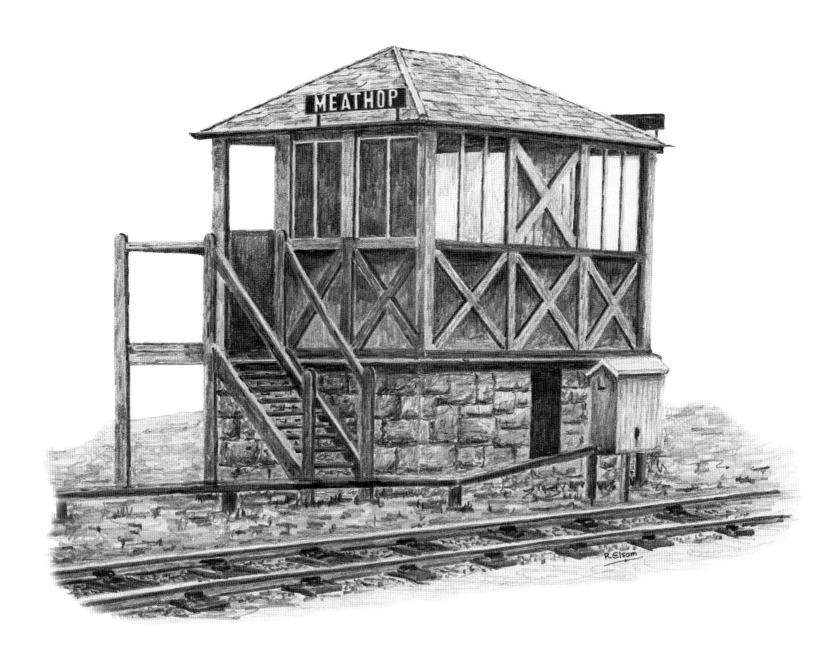

Photo: Ventnor Signal Box and Tunnel Mouth, I.O.W; The Transport Treasury

THE SIGNAL-MAN

Excerpt from the short story by Charles Dickens (1866)

"Halloa! Below there!" When he heard a voice thus calling him, he was standing at the door of his box, with a flag in his hand, furled round a short pole. One would have thought, considering the nature of the ground, that he could have not doubted from what quarter the voice came; but instead of looking up to where I stood on the top of the steep cutting nearly over his head, he turned himself about, and looked down the Line. There was something remarkable in his manner of doing so, though I could not have said for my life what. But I know it was remarkable enough to attract my notice, even though his figure was foreshortened and shadowed, down in the deep trench, and mine was high above him, so steeped in the glow of an angry sunset, that I shadowed my eyes with my hand before I saw him at all. "Halloa! Below!" From looking down the Line, he turned himself about again, and raising his eyes, saw my figure high above him. "Is there any path by which I can come down and speak to you?", I repeated my enquiry. After a pause, during which he seemed to regard me with fixed attention, he motioned with his rolled up flag towards a point on my level, some two or three hundred yards distant. I called down to him, "All right" and made for that point. There, by dint of looking closely about me, I found a zigzag descending path notched out, which I followed. The cutting was deep and unusually precipitate. It was made through a clammy stone, that became oozier and wetter as I went down. For these reasons, I found the way long enough to give me time to recall a singular air of reluctance of compulsion with which he had pointed out the path. I resumed my downward way, and stepping out upon the level of the railroad, and drawing nearer to him, saw that he was a dark sallow man, with a dark beard and rather heavy eyebrows. His post was in as solitary and dismal a place as I ever saw. On either side, a dripping-wet wall of jagged stone, excluding all view but a strip of sky; the perspective one way only a crooked prolongation of this great dungeon; the shorter perspective in the other direction terminating in a gloomy red light, and the gloomier entrance to a black tunnel, in whose massive architecture there was a barbarous, depressing, and forbidding air. So little sunlight ever found its way to this spot, that it had an earthy, deadly smell; and so much cold wind rushed through it, that it struck chill to me, as if I had left the natural world.

TAIN (SCOTLAND)

A Dutton Type I signal box built for the Highland Railway which, although serving an area with little freight traffic and few passengers, resulting in infrequent trains, some were nevertheless so heavily loaded that Highland Railway passing loops had to be long, and required a controlling signal box at each end. This box is Tain North and worked with an identical box at the southern end of the loop. This is quite a lofty all timber building, and the vertical boarding and somewhat shallow glazing to the operating floor area both seem to emphasise the overall height. Two "Ball and Spear" finials at roof ridge level, and decorative valancing to the barge boards and porch entrance add interest.

Opened 1894   Closed   Not known.

(O.S. Landranger Sht. 21   G.R. NH 7882)

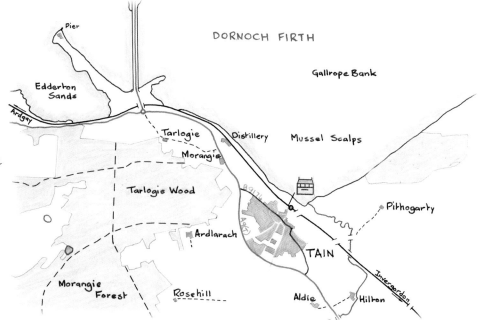

100

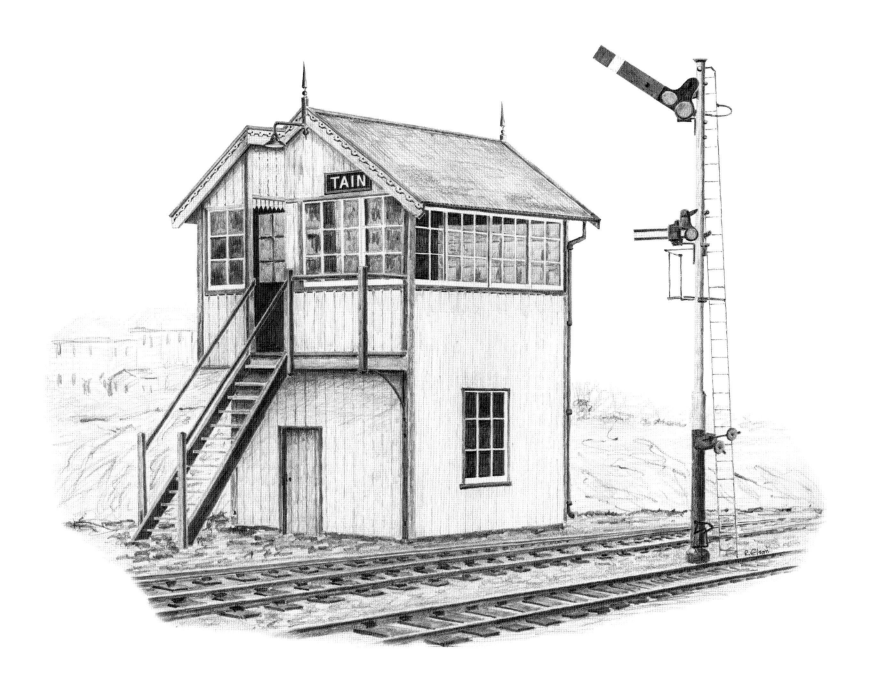

TAIN

R.Elson

WORGRET JUNCTION (DORSET)

Worgret Junction signal box dated from the opening of the line to Swanage. The lack of valancing at the fascia boards emphasises the amount of glazing which was more generous than usual as the box stood in the 'V' of the junction it protected and had windows on all four sides. It possessed typical South Western features for Type 3 boxes, such as the large wooden roof vent, and a railed cat-walk around the operating floor cabin. This box contained a Stevens frame of 16 levers and it survived for 91 years when its control of points was transferred to a five lever ground frame.

Opened 1885   Closed 1976

(O.S. Landranger Sht. 195   G.R. SY 9086)

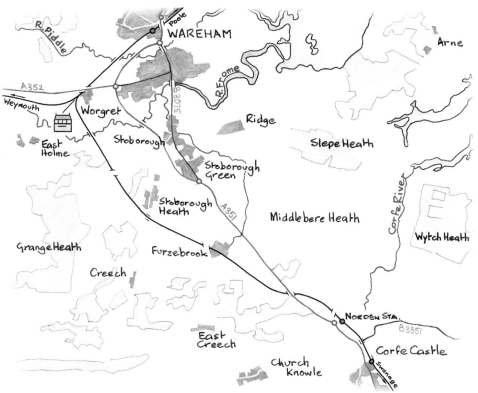

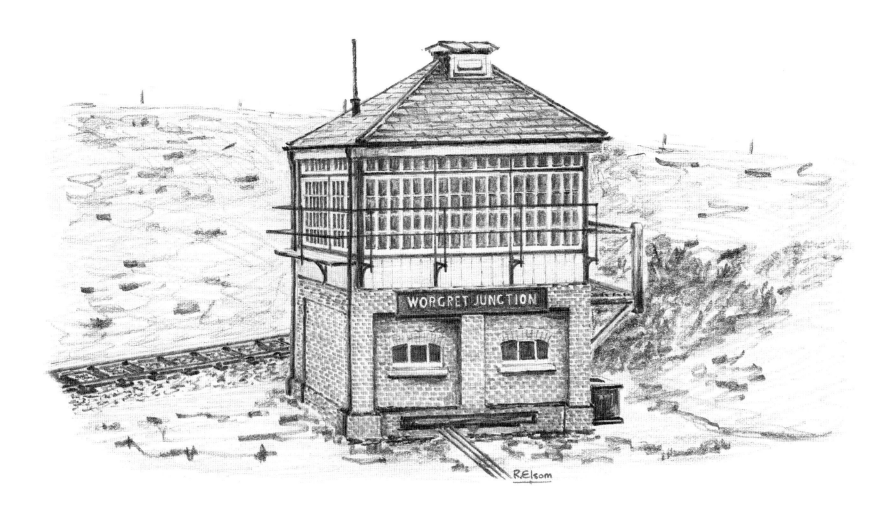

My own all too fleeting moments of time spent inside a signal box have left me with emotive memories of the impact inflicted on the senses by the unique sights, sounds and smells associated with what went on inside them. Sights of gleaming brass work, mirror-like lino-covered floors, highly polished instruments, and regimented rows of colour-coded levers; sounds of bells urgently tinging out their Morse-like messages, the distinctive clang of metal on metal as a lever is moved; a synthesis of smells, oil, floor-polish, coffee, burning coals. To me, this all seems to contribute to what I can only imagine was a commendable and enjoyable environment in which to spend one's working days, and certainly one which many a signalman must surely have been extremely sorry to lose. I cannot begin to describe what that must have been like, so it's therefore only fitting that the final words at the end of this book should be uttered by an ex-signalman.

Roger Elsom, Southampton 2023

GLAISDALE (NORTH YORKSHIRE)

This signal box on the Whitby and Battersby line, is an all brick structure situated at Glaisdale station which dates from 1865. Oddly, the box is not platform mounted, but nestles in the adjacent field. A wooden "bridge" has been provided over the point rodding and signal wires that cross the platform from box to tracks.

(O.S. Landranger Sht 94   G.R. NZ 7805)

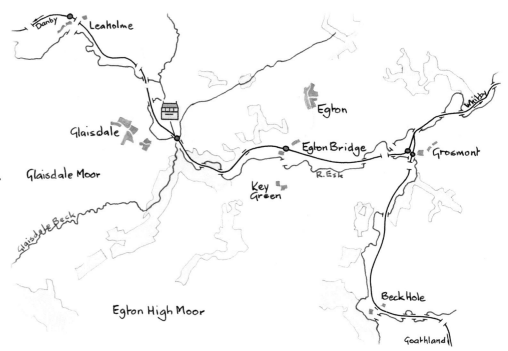

DAGGONS ROAD (DORSET)

Finding a name for this station proved to be a bit of a problem for the London and South Western Railway as the village it served, Alderholt could be, they thought, confused with Aldershot, and the only other notable nearby landmark was named Charing Cross, obviously ruling that out too. It thus transpired that a local farm received significant recognition when the L.S.W.R. decided to adopt its name for the station. Many ground level boxes came in a variety of shapes and sizes. Daggons Road was a unique structure with its unusual curved, Pagoda-like roof clad in tarred canvas. The fact that, when it was opened in 1878, standard designs were well established, the choice of this design seems strange indeed. Initially, the box contained 8 levers, but was reduced to a ground frame in 1903. Generally, where this occurred, much of the lever frame became redundant, but there were some significant changes to the track layout and 3 levers were actually added. Although seldom used in its latter years, this box remained active until the West Moors to Alderbury line closed in May 1964.

Opened 1878   Closed 1964

(O.S. Landranger Sht. 195   G.R. SU 113124)

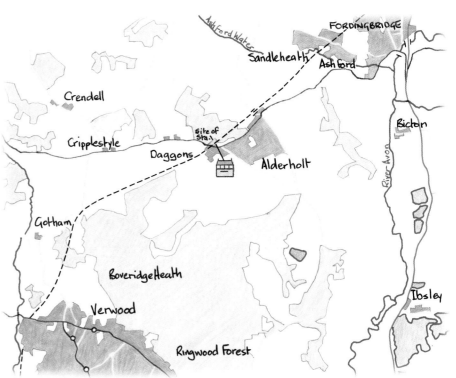

108

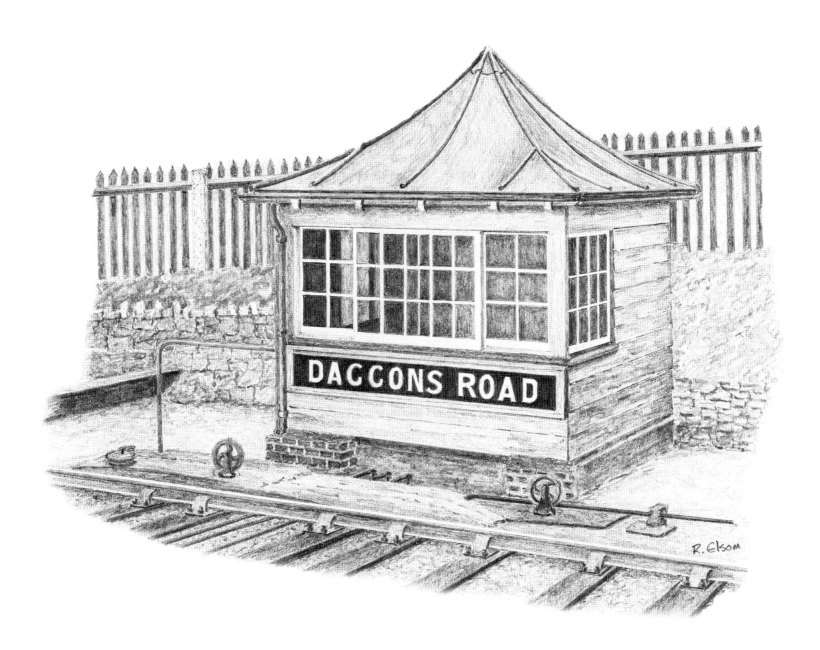

My last visit to Savernake was after the spectre of modernisation had not only reached the signal box here but passed through, leaving in its wake a trail of destruction. Where once stately signals had stood the lineside was empty, the signal box too with broken panes and I could see rusty levers. The instruments and bells ripped out and thrown away. Most of all there was no tell-tale smoke from the chimney, all was silent, the last bell had been rung.

Kevin Robertson

My thanks go firstly to my family for their continuing interest and encouragement throughout this whole project, especially my son Jon who took on the many less fulfilling, but essential administrative tasks involved. Also to Andy Cake for his original design inspiration. Finally, I am extremely grateful for the invaluable, professional advice and support given to me by Kevin Robertson of Transport Treasury Publishing.

RE

Bibliography

1. Railway Women by Helena Wojtczak
2. Dow's Dictionary of Railway Quotations by Andrew Dow
3. Resignalling Britain by Michael Rhodes
4. Signal Boxes for the Modeller by Michael A. Vanns
5. The Somerset and Dorset Railway by Robin Atthill
6. The Signal Box by The Signalling Study Group
7. Signal Boxes of the London & South Western Railway by G. A. Pryer
8. L.N.E.R Constituent Signalling by A. A. Maclean
9. Southern Signals by G .A. Pryer
10. The Somerset and Dorset in the Fifties Vol. One 1950-54 by Ivo Peters

Internet

Herstoria – A History That Puts Woman In Her Place

Mapping

Ordnance Survey 1:50,000 Landranger Series (my own representations)